Creating A Vision

By Aaron Fields

If Your Vision Is Prophesying, Please Use It In Proportion To Your Faith.

Aaron Fields

Food For Thought

"Sometimes you have to embrace solitude in order to achieve your vision."

"In life, you must find a way to manifest and cultivate your gifts."

"It's okay to have obstacles because that's part of life."

"The turning point towards success is when you decide to focus on yourself."

"If you believe you can do something
or can't do something, either way
you're right."

"Life is about creating something
that's bigger than you."

"Never talk yourself out of doing
something great."

"Don't let your enemies hinder you
from achieving success."

"If your enemies know your weakness,
they will try to distract you."

"Creating a vision will help you focus on the gifts you have."

"During tough times, always search
for the light at the end of the tunnel."

"Having a vision for yourself will prevent you from becoming an envious person."

"Most people in this world are envious of other people because they don't have what it takes to be successful."

"Just because other people don't have a vision for themselves, doesn't mean you should be like them."

"If you're not satisfied with your life,
find a way to fix it."

"Don't blame your shortcoming on someone that's doing great things."

"Keep a group of positive people around you so they can help make your vision come to life."

"Always be self-motivated."

"Never allow someone to talk you into
not believing in yourself."

"The greater the person becomes, the more focused they are."

"Being by yourself will help you get
your mind right."

"If you can't create a vision for yourself, it will never manifest."

"In order to get to any level of
fulfillment in your life, you must
believe in yourself and have a vision."

"I hope you continue to grow in your success and become the person that you want to be."

"Most people have visions for themselves, but it's never manifested because they're too busy trying to please other people."

"Embrace your vision and stop
wasting valuable time."

CPSIA information can be obtained
at www.ICGtesting.com
Printed in the USA
BVHW021337080621
609006BV00002B/20